CULTIVATE YOUR *offers*

Craft Offers That Sell With Ease Using Human Design

A companion workbook to the book, *Cultivate You!*

Lise Cartwright | HustleandGroove.com

© COPYRIGHT 2024 LISE CARTWRIGHT | HUSTLEANDGROOVE.COM

All rights reserved. No part of this publication may be reproduced, distributed, stored in a retrieval system, or transmitted in any form or by any means, including photocopying, recording, or other electronic or mechanical methods, without the prior written permission of the publisher, except in the case of brief quotations embodied in critical reviews and certain other noncommercial uses permitted by copyright law.

While the publisher and author have used their best efforts in preparing this guide and planner, they make no representations or warranties with respect to the accuracy or completeness of the contents of this document. The information is to be used at your own risk. Every situation is different and will not be an exact replica of the examples provided in this book. The author cannot guarantee results of any specific outcomes gleaned from using the methods outlined in the following pages.

You have permission to photograph this planner for your review and include any photographs or videos in your social media sharing. Please do not photograph and/or film the whole planner.

For all other permissions, please email the author:
lise@hustleandgroove.com

ISBN: 978-0-6458845-3-1

Hello Creative Business Owner

Are you ready to create a consistent income business based on what FEELS easy and fun for you?

With this workbook you will be able to create an action plan to that brings you consistent income month after month. No more feast or famine cycles for you!

You've made a great decision, here's why...

✓ Creating an online business that harnesses your strengths allows you to focus on the tactics and strategies that feel easy and fun for you. It allows you to connect with your audience in a way that comes **natural** to you. This leads to easy cash flow and no one-size-fits-all strategies in sight!

✓ When you combine your you-nique gifts, strengths, and talents to craft your messages, you're able to step into truly authentic content and offers that resonates with your people. You don't need to use fancy words or fancy tactics to attract your ideal customer. Be you. Show that you genuinely care. Empower and inspire your audience by sharing the authentic, raw you. Since you're here to truly make a difference in the lives of your people, they are much more likely to want to buy more from—and work with—someone they feel they **connect** with.

✓ On top of being easy and fun, when you focus on you doing you in your business, you're able to **sell** to your audience will ease. By leaning into being more you, you stand out in your space because you're creating offers that provide value and changes lives. Marketing your business doesn't mean you need to sell your soul. Instead, when you do what comes naturally to you, cash flows freely.

Lise Cartwright | HustleandGroove.com

Contents
it's time to discover what's inside!

Introduction — 06

CHAPTER ONE
- Tangible Offer Framework — 10

CHAPTER TWO
- Your Offer Suite — 31

CHAPTER THREE
- Launching Your Offers — 41

NOW WHAT?
- Your Next Steps — 57

About The Author — 63

Create offers that your audience wants then bake in what they need... meet them where they are at!

LISE CARTWRIGHT, BEST SELLING AUTHOR AND CREATIVE BUSINESS COACH

Your Free Gift

To make the most out of this book, download all the extra resources and trainings you've just unlocked as a thank you for buying this book!

You can access all of these via the resources hub here: www.hustleandgroove.com/cyoresources

Introduction
you do you!

Congratulations!

You made it through the discovering *you* process, IF you read the first book in the series...

Not sure what I'm talking about?

This workbook is ideally used in conjunction with the first book, *Cultivate You! Harness Your Strengths, Craft Your Message, and Market With Ease (Using Human Design)*.

If you haven't grabbed this yet, head on over to **https://www.hustleandgroove.com/cybbook** and read that first, especially if you're not familiar with Human Design.

But if you're all caught up...

I'm so proud of you.

I hope you continue to pay attention to what *feels* easy and fun for you, particularly as we transition into this workbook.

Inside, we're going to dive into tangible and practical ways you can start to apply your (Human Design) strategy and authority to your business.

And for the contents of this workbook, we're going to focus around your offers and marketing.

Let's dive in!

CHAPTER ONE

tangible offer framework

ideas...

ideas...

Tangible Offer Framework

Before you can create a marketing plan, we need to consider the way in which you create your offers.

After working with several amazing coaches and following my gut, I've developed a framework that covers a whole bunch of bases so that when we sit down to create marketing materials for our offers, the framework is already there.

Introducing the Tangible Offer Framework.

This framework takes the viewpoint of not needing us to niche down (ever) but instead, ensuring that our offers meet the needs of our customers.

But from the offer level.

Here's what I mean.

Whenever I get an idea for a new offer, before I go through the process of creating, I complete the Tangible Offer Framework first.

And I filter all the answers to the questions I'm going to share with you through the lens of the very first question… *who is the ideal customer for this offer?*

You might be thinking, *"Um, aren't we niching here, Lise?"*

In a sense, we are *niching down*, but not in the traditional way.

By being clear on **who** the ideal customer is for the offer, I'm able to speak to that person.

This doesn't mean other people won't buy the offer (because I know you're likely thinking… *but this offer works for everyone*!).

It's not about excluding; it's about helping the person that needs your offer the most to self-identify as they read your sales page.

Before we dive into the Tangible Offer Framework, it's time for a check-in.

Creating our offers in an aligned way means following our strategy first and foremost.

Here's what that looks like for each type:

MANIFESTOR: What do you feel compelled to bring to life? What's got you all buzzy and excited within? Before you release it, don't forget to inform your audience first.

GENERATOR: What external thing triggered the offer you're looking to create? What are you responding to?

MANIFESTING GENERATOR: What external thing triggered the offer you're looking to create? What's got you buzzy and excited? What are you responding to? And before you release it, inform your audience first.

PROJECTOR: What have you noticed about your audience that's inspired you to create? What do you keep getting questions about?

REFLECTOR: What have you felt drawn to bring to life during the past 28 days? What does your audience need right now?

It's important that you follow your strategy when it comes to creating your offers. If you don't, then you can experience your *not-self theme* and back yourself into a corner.

Now that we've got that out of the way, let's dive into the *Tangible Offer Framework*.

Question #1: Who is the ideal customer for this offer?
This is where you want to get really specific.

Example: *Female entrepreneurs who are sick of hearing that they need to "niche down".*

Or... *Female course creators who are tired of living in the 'feast or famine' income cycle.*

These are both my ideal customers for the Digital Income Accelerator membership.

Take a moment to identify who your **ideal customer** is for each of the offers you have (or plan to have)...

Question #2: What are the pain points/struggles/fears they have? This is your Island A - aka what life looks like for them right now.
For this question, you'll want to describe how they are feeling, what life looks like right now, what struggle town is.

There are two approaches to this.

One is to list down a bunch of bullet points for the pains they are experiencing. Ideally, these will be in their own words (not what you believe these to be).

The second way is to write this as a story.

I like to do both.

Let's look at some examples:

- *I'm struggling to figure out what offers to create and how to sell them.*
- *I'm not sure what offers to create first. Do I need a certain number of offers?*
- *How to build my email list without having to post in all the Facebook Groups.*
- *How can I market my business when I don't have a niche?*
- *How do I make money when I don't have the energy to do live challenges all the time?*

Island A Story: *Meet Cathy. She's been running her coaching membership and printable shop for just over 2 years. While she's had some success, she's not making the consistent income she needs to quit her part-time job.*

Cathy is sick of hustling her butt off to get her offers out there. While she can do all live challenges, run FB ads, and record Reels, she's tired. She feels burned-out and like a failure. She keeps seeing others doing things that are similar to her have success, but despite doing all the things, Cathy can't seem to replicate what they are.

Cathy is ready to give up. Maybe running her online business full-time just isn't her path.

These two examples are from my *Digital Income Accelerator Tangible Offer Framework* document.

exercise time

Take a moment to identify the **pain points** for your ideal customer through the lens of this offer (or what you're planning)...

Question #3: What does life look like for them once they have bought and completed your offer? This is Island B.
This is where you'll describe how they are feeling, what they have experienced, any 'a-ha' moments they might have had. Paint a picture through a story…

As with the previous question, you can either do this in bullet points or as a story or both.

The key is to ensure that whatever you do write speaks to whatever you have in Island A.

So, for each bullet point written in the previous question, you'd want to provide the solution here.

This will make sense when you look at the examples below.

Example:

- **ISLAND A: I'm struggling to figure out what offers to create and how to sell them.** *ISLAND B: I have a clear path forward to create offers that my audience wants and selling them simply happens as part of the process.*
- **ISLAND A: I'm not sure what offers to create first. Do I need a certain number of offers?** *ISLAND B: Following my HD strategy and authority allows me to create offers based on what feels easy and fun. I'm excited about what I can create and that it doesn't matter how many offers I have!*
- **ISLAND A: How to build my email list without having to post in all the Facebook Groups.** *ISLAND B: I'm excited that I can automate my list-building process as well as follow an organic approach that doesn't require me to be on social media at all!*
- **ISLAND A: How can I market my business when I don't have a niche?** *ISLAND B: I don't have to have a niche! I feel so free.*
- **ISLAND A: How do I make money when I don't have the energy to do live challenges all the time?** *ISLAND B: I don't have to do anything I don't want to. Instead, I can set up automated systems that meet my audience where they are at. I simply present the opportunity for people to buy from me and continue to do what's easy and fun for me. I feel light.*

Island B Story: *Meet Cathy. She just finished building out her Discoverable Content and Evergreen Sales system.*

When she first joined the Digital Income Accelerator, she wasn't sure that she'd see the success that others had experienced, but she honestly couldn't believe it.

In the 90 days since joining, Cathy has made more income than the previous 90 days but has worked fewer hours. She's also close to her goal of being able to quit her part-time job and go full-time in her business, a dream she's had for the past 2 years.

The biggest a-ha came from when Lise did Cathy's HD chart reading. Cathy hadn't even realized that she'd been allowing her open head center to run the show.

Cathy now understands how she's designed to market her business as a Generator and is excited for the next 90 days.

Following her joy has never felt easier!

Whether you do the bullet points or the story, the key is to make sure that Island A and B make sense together.

Take a moment to address **Island B** for your ideal customer based on what life looks like for them after taking your offer...

Question #4: What is the tangible result you're helping them achieve with this offer?

If someone were to ask you what the most important thing was once someone completed your offer, what would that be? This is about clearly articulating the result. Use feeling words and phrases that elicit an emotional response from your ideal customer.

There are a few frameworks I like to use with my members to help them come up with a result that makes it easy for their audience to exclaim, "This is for me!".

Framework 1: How to [result they want] without [thing they don't wanna do]

Example: How to take one bestselling offer and repurpose it into 10+ new products without having to create from scratch.

Offer Title: Magic Micro Offers

Framework 2: Create a [result they want] that [bigger result they want] in [timeframe]

Example: Create a money-making marketing plan (using human design) that brings in $5k+ per month in 90 days or less...

Offer Title: The Digital Income Accelerator membership.

This is where many of my members struggle.

They struggle because they don't have clarity on the first three questions. Once you've nailed those, the tangible result statement (which is typically the main headline on your sales page) becomes easier to craft.

Question #5: What are the key milestones/quick wins along the way? How can you break down the steps of the journey to achieve the result?
This question is about helping your ideal customer see that they are making progress.

By breaking down the result into measurable steps or milestones, your ideal customer can see the journey.

You might only have two steps; you might have nine. As long as there's progression toward the main goal of the offer, that's what counts.

Example (taken from the D.I.A sales page):

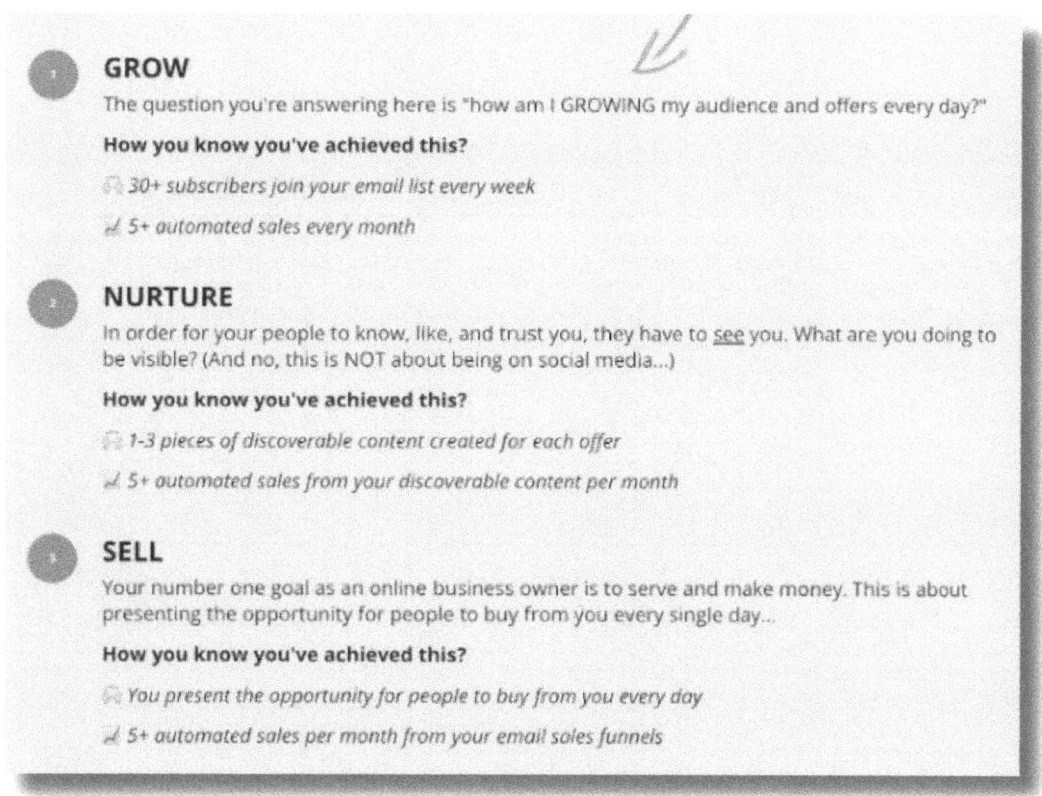

Take a moment to write down the **key milestones/wins** along the way so your ideal customer knows they are making progress...

Question #6: What is the best container (or best way to deliver) for this offer? Or What tangible deliverables can I include?

You might already have an idea of the type of container this offer is going to be presented in, but in case you don't, here are some ideas to get the ball rolling.

Marketing container ideas:

- Live workshop (or pre-recorded)
- Self-study course
- Mini-training
- Group coaching program
- Membership
- Subscription
- Mastermind
- Book
- Workbook/planner/journal

Once you've chosen the container, consider the tangible deliverables that you will also include.

For example, if you were doing a workshop (live or pre-recorded) you might have the following tangible deliverables included:

- Downloadable workbook
- Workshop slides
- Individual worksheets
- Tech tutorials
- Idea prompts

Again, this is where following your strategy and authority is needed. What do you feel called to create? What would benefit your audience?

Remember: There is no right or wrong way to deliver an offer. Focus on what feels easy and fun for you.

exercize time

Take a moment to write down the **container/tangible deliverables** you'll have in place to deliver this content...

Question #7: What do you need your ideal customer for this offer to know or understand before they buy?
This question is one of the most important questions you'll need to address in your sales copy.

This will go on your sales page, FAQs section, and in your sales emails.

Consider your ideal customer for this offer.

What misconceptions do they currently hold about the tangible result you're promising?

What beliefs do they have that might stop them from buying your offer?

What do they believe about themselves that might make them go, "I can't do this"?

To be clear: We are *not* here to *convince* our audience to buy our offers. That's not up to us.

Our responsibility is to ensure that we help them decide. Yes or no. That's it.

We help our audience decide by providing them with all the information they need to make that decision. And we do that by addressing their fears, their beliefs, concerns, and misconceptions they might have.

Because if you don't address their objections, it will most certainly lead to a no for a large portion of the people landing on your offer sales page.

So, don't skip this question.

Cultivate Your Offers Workbook

exercise time

Take a moment to write down the **misconceptions/misplaced beliefs** your ideal customers might have that could stop them from buying your offer (and how you'll address them)...

Question #8: How can you make this a no-brainer for your ideal customer?

What price will your offer be?

How will you 'value stack' this offer?

What bonuses could you include?

This final question is about helping your ideal customer make the final decision: to buy or not.

Your ideal customer will always be looking for the price early on when looking at your sales page. So don't hide it.

Price your offer based on what FEELS aligned for you.

If you have an open heart center, you will want to pay attention to any limiting beliefs that come up when considering pricing.

The not-self theme of an open heart center is a tendency to undervalue yourself and your offers.

Follow your inner authority when choosing pricing.

Value stacking is all about the tangible deliverables you're including with your offer. It can also include the bonuses (if any).

You don't always need to include bonuses.

But here's how you make that decision.

Review the previous question. What beliefs, fears, misconceptions stand in the way of your ideal customer's decision to take up this offer?

What relevant bonus content could you include/create that would override their objections?

Here's some questions to get your ideas flowing:

1. *What does your ideal customer believe they need to have in place before they are ready to buy your offer?*
2. *What resources does your ideal customer need to be successful with your offer?*
3. *What does your ideal customer need after they finish your offer to have continued success?*

You could class these ideas into buckets: before, during, and after…

Once you've finished the Tangible Offer Framework, you're ready to create your offer… but I'd recommend holding off doing so until you work your way through the rest of this section.

Cultivate Your Offers Workbook

Take a moment to identify how you'll make this a **no brainer offer** for your ideal customer. Consider bonus trainings (before and after)…

In the next chapter, we're going to look at your offer suite.

I find that by mapping out your offer suite, you'll get a clear picture of where your business is at, and where you want to take it.

This offer suite is never set in stone.

My offer suite changes quarterly. As a Manifesting Generator, I need a lot of flexibility in my business and my offer suite reflects that.

I want to give you permission to create an offer suite that feels easy and fun for you right now, with the knowledge that you can change it whenever you want.

It's always up to you.

Let's dive in.

CHAPTER TWO

your offer suite

ideas...

Mapping Out Your Offer Suite

Building your offer suite is very much an exercise in following your strategy and authority.

Here are some prompts to help keep you on track based on your type. Consider these as we move through this chapter:

MANIFESTORS: What do you feel compelled to create? Make sure you inform your audience before you decide to move forward with an offer.

GENERATORS: What are you noticing? What patterns do you see? What questions are you being asked? Remember, you need to create in response to external stimuli.

MANIFESTING GENERATORS: What patterns do you notice in your business? What do your analytics tell you? What questions are you being asked or noticing? Remember, you need to create in response to external stimuli then inform your audience before you move forward with the offer.

PROJECTORS: What is the best way for you to share your zone of genius? What would you create without attachment to the outcome? Your strategy is to wait for the invitation. What have you been invited to recently? What questions are you being asked? What questions do you want to answer?

REFLECTORS: What have you experienced in the last 30 days that you continue to be excited and energized about? Remember, you don't make decisions quickly. Experience things, feel things, and ultimately, do what feels good to you.

Remember: creating offers is about meeting your audience where they are at and baking in what they need. How you choose to do that will be based on your strategy and authority...

I'm a visual person, so my offer suite is mapped out inside Canva. You can see my offer suite and a video walk-through of this here.

When creating your own offer suite, it helps to think about a few things first.

> **YOUR OFFERS**
>
> #1: *How much money do you want to make each month?*
>
> #2: *What type of business model allows you to live your desired lifestyle?*

Let's start with the first question.

If you already have some offers and you've been in business for a year or more, then you likely already know the number you want to make each month.

The question is: *are you achieving that?*

If you're not, then we need to look at your numbers:

- How many people do you have on your email list?
- How often do you present the opportunity for them to buy from you?
- What's the open rate on your sales emails?
- What's the click rate on your sales emails?
- What's the price of your offer(s)?
- Do you use order bumps and upsells?

Let's use a fictional example so that you can understand what to do with this data...

Cathy is an online coach.

Here's her numbers:

Number of people on my email list	1,237
How often do I sell to my email list?	Once a month
Average open rate on my sales emails	25%
Average click rate on my sales emails	1%
Price of my offer(s)	Membership $37/m Mini-Course $27 Template $9
I use order bumps (but don't use upsells)	When people buy my membership, my mini-course is the order bump

Based on this information, here's what it likely looks like for Cathy right now:

Once a month, Cathy sends out a sales email to her email list. 25% of those people are opening that email. That means that 309 people actually see her sales email.

Of the 309 people that open her sales email, 1% of those people are clicking through to her sales page. That's only three people.

Already, I can see where some gaps are for Cathy.

Depending on her strategy, I would advise her as follows…

MANIFESTOR: If Cathy was a Manifestor, I'd suggest that she emails her audience more often, sharing what's going on inside her membership, or successes her current customers are having with her offers.

Anytime Cathy wants to run a special promotion, I'd also recommend that she gives her audience a 'heads-up' by sending an email letting them know what's happening and when.

I'd likely also recommend that Cathy implement the Evergreen Sales System so that her sales process was automated.

GENERATOR: If Cathy was a Generator, I'd first ask her if she had created her offers in response. I'd then recommend (depending on that answer) that she either survey her audience to find out what they need help with right now and/or get her to look at her analytics to see what content her audience has been engaging with the most.

From there, I'd recommend that Cathy do some live promotions, like running a 3-day challenge or hosting a live round of her mini-course.

I'd also recommend that Cathy create Discoverable Content for her offers so that as her audience is searching for solutions, her content would serve up the solutions.

MANIFESTING GENERATOR: If Cathy were a Mani Gen, I'd first ask her if she had created her offers in response and also informed her audience before she launched them.

I'd then recommend (depending on that answer) that she either survey her audience to find out what they need help with right now and/or get her to look at her analytics to see what content her audience has been engaging with the most.

From there, I'd recommend that Cathy ask her audience what they would like the most — a live round of her mini-course or a live challenge or whatever she decided to offer.

I'd also recommend that Cathy create Discoverable Content for her offers so that as her audience is searching for answers to their problems, her content would serve up the solutions.

PROJECTOR: If Cathy was a Projector, I'd first ask her if she had created her offers based on her zone of genius. I'd also ask if she created based on what she noticed her audience struggling with.

From there, I'd recommend that Cathy shows up for her audience on a regular basis where she shares her insights, knowledge, and wisdom on a regular basis. This ideally would be via email, but if she was into social media, she would also share that content there. This content would always include a link to check out her offer(s).

I'd also recommend that Cathy create Discoverable Content for her offers so that as her audience is searching for solutions, her content would serve up the solutions. I'd also recommend that she set up the Evergreen Sales System to automate her sales process.

REFLECTOR: If Cathy was a Reflector, I'd ask her how often she was emailing her audience. What her engagement was like. Based on her response, I'd recommend emailing her audience more often, based on her reflections, what she was noticing around her and her audience.

I'd then recommend that she create Discoverable Content for her offers and set up the Evergreen Sales System to automate her sales process. This would free Cathy up to focus on following her energy ebb and flow, while not having to worry about making money (because that would be taken care of with the two systems she has set up).

Once you're clear on your numbers, the next step is to ensure that your business model aligns with the lifestyle you're looking to create.

For example, if you want to have fewer human interactions, you're not going to be doing one-on-one coaching. You might enjoy a subscription model or a business where you focus on selling self-study courses.

If, on the other hand, you do enjoy human contact, then you'll likely enjoy hosting group coaching programs like bootcamps, challenges, or memberships.

For example, I class myself as an author and creative business coach.

I do both group coaching and 1-on-1 coaching and have several self-study courses. I also sell books, workbooks, journals, notebooks, and printables.

My offer suite is diverse because that's what works for me.

You do what works for you.

Here's a quick overview of the coaching portion of my offer suite shown below *(I have 43+ books, so it's a little hard to have them all in one place!)*:

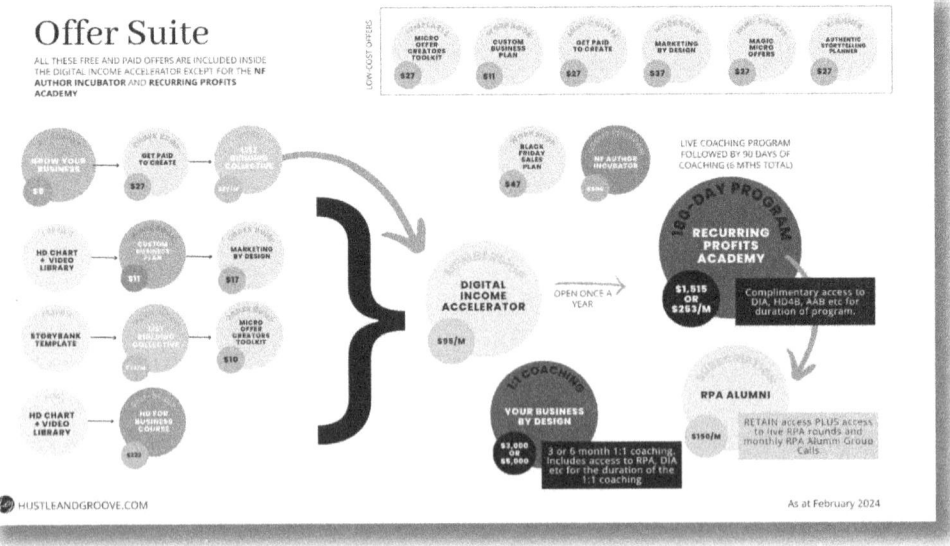

Take a moment to reflect on your current business model.

Does it align with you energetically?

Did you follow your strategy and authority when you made the decision to create the business you now have?
Are you doing what feels easy and fun for you?

Once you've got some answers, then you can map out your offer suite to better reflect the business and income you're looking to have.

One thing that I want to address (because you might be thinking it) is that you don't need to have high ticket offers if they don't align, or if you're not ready for them yet.

It's more about having a business that's easy and fun for you. When you do that, your income grows with ease.

RESOURCE: Offer Suite Template and Income Projection Calculator (available inside the resources hub).

In the next chapter, we're going to look at what it looks like to launch your offers based on your type, or what's easy and fun for you.

Let's dive in.

ideas...

CHAPTER THREE
launching offers

ideas...

Launching Your Offers

When it comes to launching our offers, it's important that we ensure that we've followed our strategy and authority in creating them.

> **LAUNCHING**
>
> **Let's define launching:** *Launching occurs when you're bringing a brand new offer to the world. Once something is out in the world, you are no longer launching it, you're simply promoting it.*

I believe this is what causes a lot of heartache for us creative entrepreneurs. We feel like we always have to be launching something new.

But we don't. Not unless we're following our strategy and authority.

So let's assume you have a new offer you want to launch.

Jot down your initial thoughts on HOW you might launch based on what *feels* easy and fun for you.

Launching Offers as a...

MANIFESTOR

You're designed to initiate. To create movement. You don't have constant energy, it comes to you in surges. You're at 200% when you're following your urges, doing and creating. Once that urge is fulfilled, your energy will drop so that you can rest and prepare for your next surge of energy.

What are you excited about bringing to the world? Following your authority, what feels energetically aligned?

INFORM your audience once you've decided. A quick email, post on social media... keep it casual but show your excitement and let them know more details will follow.

This might look like this:

"Hey lovely! I'm super excited to let you know that I'm working on this amazing 6-week bootcamp for you right now.

I can't share all the details with you just yet, but I wanted to let you know you can expect to learn more about it next week.

Stay tuned!"

Potential launching ideas for Manifestors:

- Hosting a live 3-day challenge
- Hosting a short, transformational workshop that then invites people to your offer
- A series of live videos on your fav social platform

The whole point of launching is to get people to buy your offer. The more INFORMING you do (sharing why you're excited, what's involved, what they can expect) the faster people will sign up!

Launching Offers as a... Manifestor

Take a moment to jot down your ideas about how you might launch your next offer based on how you're feeling, what you're excited about, and how you plan to INFORM your audience. Remember – follow your energy. If you're feeling low-energy, keep things low-energy!

Launching Offers as a...

GENERATOR

You're designed to follow your joy. To only do the things that light you up. Everything you commit to is based on what your gut tells you it's excited about. You're here to generate good energy. Your energy is consistent and sustainable only when you're doing things that light you up, that you're excited about.

You can launch however you wish... as long as you're responding to something external. How are you responding right now?

What is your gut telling you? What brings you joy? What do you notice your audience struggling with?

You're designed to create in response, so once you've got an idea that you're gut confirms is a 'heck yes', follow these steps:

Step 1: What is the external thing you're responding to? Something your audience has been talking about? Did they ask you specifically for something? Or did you notice someone else doing something and your gut lit up?

- If you CANNOT find an external prompt that triggered the idea, then you need to step into waiting to respond. You do that by simply asking the Universe to send you signs that the idea you've got is yours to move forward with then you WAIT. Pay attention to what reminds you about your idea...
- If you CAN find the external prompt that triggered your idea, then you can move to the next step.

Step 2: Following your authority, what feels energetically aligned? If you have EMOTIONAL authority, you'll need to sleep on it. If you have SACRAL authority, follow your gut.

Step 3: Where does your audience fit into the mix? In other words, is this something that they are asking for / struggling with / talking about? If you're not sure, you can simply provide some options to your audience (a survey perhaps) and then respond from there.

Launching Offers as a...

GENERATOR

You're designed to follow your joy. To only do the things that light you up. Everything you commit to is based on what your gut tells you it's excited about. You're here to generate good energy. Your energy is consistent and sustainable only when you're doing things that light you up, that you're excited about.

Potential launching ideas for Generators:

- Pre-recorded short videos that break down your offer step-by-step

- Your unique way of storytelling and helping your audience make a decision – yes or no

- A series of posts on your fav social platform

The whole point of launching is to present the opportunity for people to buy from you when they are ready. If you've created in response, your audience will let you know by buying what you're offering.

Launching Offers as a... Generator

Take a moment to jot down your ideas about how you might launch your next offer based on what you're responding to. What feels joyful right now for you?

Launching Offers as a...

MANI GEN

Are designed to chart a different path, to follow all the twists and turns they feel drawn to investigate. You are a multi-passionate person. Your energy is spontaneous and in the moment. Just because you can doesn't mean you should...

You can launch however you wish... as long as you're responding to something external. How are you responding right now? How will you inform your audience?

What are you noticing that lights up your gut? What do you see your audience struggling with? You're designed to create in response then inform, so once you've got an idea that you're gut confirms is a 'heck yes', follow these steps:

Step 1: What is the external thing you're responding to? Something your audience has been talking about? Did they ask you specifically for something? Or did you notice someone else doing something and your gut lit up?

- If you CANNOT find an external prompt that triggered the idea, then you need to step into waiting to respond. You do that by simply asking the Universe to send you signs that the idea you've got is yours to move forward with then you WAIT. Pay attention.
- If you CAN find the external prompt that triggered your idea, then you can move to the next step.

Step 2: Following your authority, what feels energetically aligned? If you have EMOTIONAL authority, you'll need to sleep on it. If you have SACRAL authority, follow your gut.

Step 3: Where does your audience fit into the mix? In other words, is this something that they are asking for / struggling with / talking about? If you're not sure, you can simply provide some options to your audience (a survey perhaps) and then respond from there.

Step 4: If you are certain on your offer, you need to also INFORM your audience. Send a short email, post on socials, wherever you do to connect with your audience. Keep it short and brief and let them know more details will follow (or you could also simply give them a few choices to choose from too).

Launching Offers as a...

MANI GEN — *Are designed to chart a different path, to follow all the twists and turns they feel drawn to investigate. You are a multi-passionate person. Your energy is spontaneous and in the moment. Just because you can doesn't mean you should...*

Potential launching ideas for Manifesting Generators:

- Live challenge or bootcamp where you help your people achieve something and invite them to the next step with you

- A short video on your sales page coupled with storytelling emails

- A series of live videos on your fav social platform

The whole point of launching is to present the opportunity for people to buy from you when they are ready. If you've created in response and informed, your audience will let you know by buying what you're offering.

Launching Offers as a... Manifesting Generator

Take a moment to jot down your ideas about how you might launch your next offer based on what you're responding to. What feels joyful right now for you?

Cultivate Your Offers Workbook

Launching Offers as a...

PROJECTOR

Are designed to see things in a way that others can't. You're here to help everyone work and function better once you master this for yourself. You don't have a consistent energy source, but you don't need it. Your energy is efficient and able to achieve more in a few hours than others can in the same amount of time.

You can launch however you wish... as long as you've been invited to share your offers with your audience. How have you been invited?

What conversations have you been having where you've been able to clearly see EXACTLY what the problem and solution is?

You're designed to wait for the invitation, so once you've identified what you want to offer, follow these steps:

1. Following your authority, what feels energetically aligned to move forward with? Remember, if you have EMOTIONAL or MENTAL authority, you'll need to give yourself 24-48 hours to sort through what you're feeling.
2. Once you've decided on your offer, write down 3-4 ideas for content (Discoverable Content) around your offer that showcases your expertise... things like conversations you've had where you haven't been able to provide your advice, solutions you've implemented with clients, insights you've gleaned from working with your audience etc.
3. If the offer is an existing offer, set up an interest/waitlist page and point your audience to that from your Discoverable Content.
4. If the offer is not existing, consider pre-selling your offer with a waitlist page and sales email sequence.

Potential launching ideas for Projectors (once you've been invited):

- Pre-recorded challenge or bootcamp where you help your people achieve something and invite them to the next step with you

- Daily posts/videos that invite people to join your waitlist

The whole point of launching is to present the opportunity for people to buy from you once they have invited you to do so. If you've been sharing your Discoverable Content and invited people to join your waitlist, your audience will let you know by buying what you're offering.

Launching Offers as a... Projector

Take a moment to jot down your ideas about how you might launch your next offer based on what feels energetically aligned. Once you've got people onto the waitlist, what content do you need to share with them to help them make a decision – yes or no?

Launching Offers as a...

> **REFLECTOR**
>
> *Are designed to pick up on everything. You are a mirror for your audience, reflecting directly back to them who they are and what they struggle with, but also what they are great at. You don't have a set energy level, it ebbs and flows based on the lunar cycle. This is why it's important to place yourself in the best environments.*

You can launch however you wish. If you want to get things done, surround yourself with energetic people.

What conversations have you been having where you've been SURPRISED by what you discovered? What is your audience doing that's making you feel curious?

You're designed to wait a lunar cycle, so once you've identified what you want to offer, follow these steps:

1. Ideally, you won't be bringing anything new to the world. You'll want to be promoting something that already exists (otherwise you'll need to wait 28-29 days to bring your idea to fruition).
2. Looking at the transits for the next two weeks, what gates and centers will be activated for you? This will help you determine your energy and what natural gifts you can lean into during this time.
3. Once you've decided on your offer, write down 3-4 ideas for content (Discoverable Content) around your offer that busts any myths / misconceptions / incorrect beliefs your audience has about your offer.
4. Set up an interest/waitlist page for the offer, putting the approx. date of when you're planning to 'open doors'.
5. Follow your flow!

Potential launching ideas for Reflectors:

- Pre-recorded challenge or bootcamp where you help your people achieve something and invite them to the next step with you
- Pre-scheduled daily posts/videos that invite people to join your waitlist or send them straight to your sales page

The whole point of launching is to present the opportunity for people to buy from you. If you've been sharing your Discoverable Content and invited people to join your waitlist or straight to your sales page, your audience will let you know by buying what you're offering.

Launching Offers as a... Reflector

Take a moment to jot down your ideas about how you might launch your next offer based on what feels energetically aligned. Once you've got people onto the waitlist, what content do you need to share with them to help them make a decision – yes or no?

ideas...

ideas...

Success seems to be connected with action. Successful people keep moving. They make mistakes, but they don't quit.

CONRAD HILTON

NOW WHAT?
your next steps...

ideas...

You Made It!
what to do next...

By now, this workbook + planning guide should be full to the brim with your ideas, creative thoughts, answers to your burning questions and as many scribbles as needed to get you to this point.

My intention with this workbook was to provide you with the space to explore some additional concepts not covered inside the first book in this series, **Cultivate You!** Harness Your Strengths, Craft Your Message, and Market With Ease!

It does get to be easy and fun… AND profitable!

Once you've completed all the exercises, all that's left is to take action, create your launch plan based on what feels energetically aligned (while also following your strategy) and then implement. You'll learn how to do even more of this inside the next workbook, *Cultivate Your Cashflow...*

You can find that on Amazon here:
https://www.hustleandgroove.com/cycashflow

Or you could simply check out the entire **Cultivate Your Business Series** and pick the book that best meets your needs right now.

You Made It!
what to do next...

You'll find those here: **https://www.hustleandgroove.com/cybseries**

You might also be starting to feel #allthefeels... and a few new fears, challenges, and limiting beliefs are rearing their ugly heads.

It's likely that these are centered around the selling of your offers. You're probably judging yourself, thinking: *"Who will buy what I've created?"*

Or you might be experiencing decision fatigue, overwhelm, and plain ole *"I don't know what to do!"* syndrome.

If that's you, then you might like to check out the step-by-step roadmap that walks you through an additional way of approaching all of this, with video and audio training coupled with templates, swipe copy and more.

It's the exact process I took to get to consistent $5k months, all while following my strategy and authority...

And if you didn't get a chance to check out the resources hub, where you'll find extra resources + trainings to help you further with this book, make sure you visit **www.hustleandgroove.com/cyoresources**.

Good luck with it all and thanks so much for sharing your knowledge and expertise with the world.

We need people like you sharing what they know.

I'd also love it if you took this time to leave a review on Amazon. You can let me know what you liked and what you didn't like right there.

Or alternatively, shoot me an email with your feedback: lise@hustleandgroove.com.

And remember, you got this!

It does get to be easy and fun in your business... you just gotta figure out what that looks like for you.

LISE CARTWRIGHT

About The Author
meet Lise Cartwright

Lise Cartwright is a bestselling author and creative business coach who is obsessed with helping others create and grow a business and life they love!

She loves curling up on a comfy couch with a good book, a hot cup of Chai Latte, and the soothing sounds of waves crashing against the white sandy beaches of the Gold Coast, Australia.

She's the founder of **www.hustleandgroove.com**, the #1 online resource for getting clear on your business model and growing an online business you are excited to work in. Her business motto is: *"if it's not easy and fun, why do it?!"*

Through her books, training videos, and coaching, she's helped thousands of people on their journey to creating an online business that's **easy**, **fun**, and **profitable**.

You can connect with Lise on the following social media platforms:

 FACEBOOK.COM/HUSTLEANDGROOVE

 LINKEDIN.COM/IN/LISECARTWRIGHT

 INSTAGRAM.COM/LISECARTWRIGHTNZ

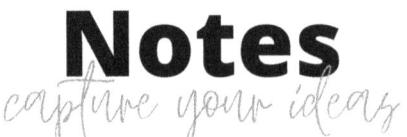

Notes
capture your ideas

Notes
capture your ideas

Notes
capture your ideas